Spiritual Intermediality and Spiritual Emblematics
in the Early Modern Period

Johann Anselm Steiger

SPIRITUAL INTERMEDIALITY AND SPIRITUAL EMBLEMATICS IN THE EARLY MODERN PERIOD[1]

MEDIA THEORETICAL AND HISTORICAL-THEOLOGICAL FOUNDATIONS

1 Funded by the Deutsche Forschungsgemeinschaft (DFG, German Research Foundation) 435118611 – Research Unit 5138 Spiritual Intermediality in the Early Modern Period, Subproject 1. The following article is based on a part of the introduction to the following work: Johann Anselm Steiger, *Emblematik in Sakralbauten des Ostseeraums*, 8 vols., Geistliche Intermedialität in der Frühen Neuzeit / Spiritual Intermediality in the Early Modern Period 2–9 (Regensburg: Schnell & Steiner, 2023), here 1:7–37.

Bibliographic information published by the Deutsche Nationalbibliothek:
The Deutsche Nationalbibliothek lists this publication in the Deutsche Nationalbibliografie; detailed bibliographic data are available on the Internet at https://dnb.de

1st edition 2024
© 2024 Verlag Schnell & Steiner GmbH, Leibnizstraße 13, 93055 Regensburg, Germany
Layout: typegerecht berlin
Printed in Germany

ISBN 978-3-7954-3911-8
E-ISBN 978-3-7954-3912-5 (PDF)
DOI https://doi.org/10.61035/3795439125

The book is published open access.

Further information about our publications can be found under:
www.schnell-und-steiner.de.

TABLE OF CONTENTS

INTRODUCTION

If one studies the early modern spiritual *ars emblematica*, in particular book-external emblematics within sacred buildings,[2] a highly attractive and broad field of research opens up. There are numerous emblematic programs on pulpits, altars, galleries, pews, confessionals, patronage boxes, funeral chapels, etc. that have survived.[3] The exploration of the book-external cycles of symbols is particularly revealing if one considers them as a specific concretion of early modern intermediality,[4] namely spiritual intermediality,[5] and pays the necessary attention to their contexts within the history of images, theology, piety, preaching, and scholarship. The aim is to decipher the media-combinatorics of emblematic artefacts in ecclesiastical spaces, i. e., the horizontal-intermedial interplay of their textual and pictorial components. On the one hand, it is indispensable to compare book-external emblemata with the intermediality determining the respective printed templates. This may well be accentuated differently, either because the *picturae* in question are accompanied by longer or more

---

2 On this, see Michael Schilling, "Emblematik außerhalb des Buches," *Internationales Archiv für Sozialgeschichte der deutschen Literatur* 11 (1986): 149–174. Peter M. Daly and Hans Josef Böker, eds., *The Emblem and Architecture. Studies in Applied Emblematics from the Sixteenth to the Eighteenth Centuries*, Imago figurata studies 2 (Turnhout: Brepols, 1999). Gerhard F. Strasser and Mara Wade, eds., *Die Domänen des Emblems. Außerliterarische Anwendungen der Emblematik*, Wolfenbütteler Arbeiten zur Barockforschung 39 (Wiesbaden: Harrassowitz, 2004). Carsten-Peter Warncke, *Symbol, Emblem, Allegorie. Die zweite Sprache der Bilder* (Köln: Deubner Verlag für Kunst, Theorie & Praxis, 2005). Sabine Mödersheim, "The Emblem in the Context of Architecture," in *Emblem Scholarship. Directions and Developments. A Tribute to Gabriel Hornstein*, ed. Peter M. Daly, Imago figurata studies 5 (Turnhout: Brepols, 2005), 159–175. Simon McKeown, *Emblematic Paintings from Sweden's Age of Greatness. Nils Bielke and the Neo-stoic Gallery in Skokloster*, Imago figurata studies 6 (Turnhout: Brepols, 2006). Ignacio Arellano and Ana Martínez Pereira, eds., *Emblemática y religión en la Península Ibérica (Siglo de Oro)*, Biblioteca Áurea Hispánica 63 (Frankfurt a. M. and Madrid: Vervuert, 2010). Hartmut Freytag, Wolfgang Harms, Michael Schilling, *Gesprächskultur des Barock. Die Embleme der Bunten Kammer im Herrenhaus Ludwigsburg bei Eckernförde* (Kiel: Ludwig, 2001; 2nd ed. 2004). Wolfgang Harms et al., eds., *SinnBilderWelten. Emblematische Medien in der Frühen Neuzeit. Ausstellungskatalog* (München: Institut für Deutsche Philologie der Ludwig-Maximilians-Universität, 1999). Johannes Köhler, *Angewandte Emblematik im Fliesensaal von Wrisbergholzen bei Hildesheim* (Hildesheim: A. Lax, 1988). Wolfgang Harms and Hartmut Freytag, eds., *Außerliterarische Wirkungen barocker Emblembücher. Emblematik in Ludwigsburg, Gaarz und Pommersfelden* (München: W. Fink, 1975). On the specifically extra-literary spiritual emblematics, cf. Johann Anselm Steiger, Michael Schilling, Stefanie Arend, *Sinnbilder im Sakralraum. Die Kirche in Lucklum – Ein Kompendium der geistlichen Emblematik der Frühen Neuzeit* (Regensburg: Schnell & Steiner, 2020). Erik A. Nielsen, *Gådetale. Emblemer, symbolik, spejle. Billed-sprog IV* (Kopenhagen: Gyldendal, 2018). Hans Westphal, *Sehnsucht nach dem himmlischen Jerusalem. Das Emblemprogramm der Stettener Schlosskapelle (1682)* (Stuttgart: Kohlhammer, 2017). Radosław Grześkowiak and Jakub Niedźwiedź, "Wstęp," in *Emblematy. Wydali i opracowali Radosław Grześkowiak i Jakub Niedźwiedź. Redakcja naukowa tomu Dariusz Chemperek*, ed. Mikołaj Mieleszko, Humanizm. Polonika 6 (Warschau: Wydawnietwo Nerriton, 2010), 7–70. Cornelia Kemp, *Angewandte Emblematik in süddeutschen Barockkirchen*, Kunstwissenschaftliche Studien 53 (München and Berlin: Deutscher Kunstverlag, 1981). Carme López Calderón, *Applied Emblems in the Cathedral of Lugo. European Sources for a Spanish Cycle Addressed to the Virgin Mary*, Brill's Studies on Art, Art History, and Intellectual History 51 (Leiden and Boston: Brill, 2021). Cf., moreover, the following smaller studies: Cornelia Kemp, "Cycles d'emblèmes dans les églises de l'Allemagne du Sud au XVIIIᵉ siècle," in *Figures du Baroque*, ed. Jean-Marie Benoist (Paris: PUF, 1983), 57–72. Carsten-Peter Warncke, "Die Seele am Kreuz. Emblematische Erbauungsliteratur und geistliche Bildkunst am Beispiel eines Dekorationsprogramms

texts in the printed media, or because simplifications or differentiations, variations or sharpenings of the pictorial compositions were made in the book-external emblemata – often also through the transformation of the monochrome models into polychrome paintings. On the other hand, to decipher book-external emblemata appropriately, the reconstruction of the above-mentioned contexts in the history of images, theology, piety, preaching, and scholarship is also informative, the relevant sources of which are themselves often intermedial in character.

Of course, it is also necessary to pay attention to the arrangement of the intermedial emblem cycles in the respective ecclesiastical spaces as well as to the ephemeral concretions of intermediality that have regularly occurred or are occurring here – for example, when the Lord's Supper is celebrated at an altar decorated with emblems and the elements of bread and wine, understood as a means of salvation, are served, accompanied by spoken word, liturgical song, and possibly organ music, and in this way ephemeral, i.e., situational-worship intermediality is combined with the

im ehem. Kloster St. Peter im Schwarzwald," in *Litteratura laicorum. Beiträge zur christlichen Kunst*, ed. Heimo Reinitzer, Vestigia bibliae 2 (Hamburg: F. Wittig, 1980), 159–202. Carsten-Peter Warncke, "Allegorese als Gesellschaftsspiel. Erörternde Embleme auf dem Satz Nürnberger Silberbecher aus dem Jahre 1621," *Anzeiger des Germanischen Nationalmuseums. Nürnberg* (1982): 43–69. Dietrich Donat, "Die Kreuzgangembleme des Augustiner-Chorherrenstiftes Wettenhausen," in *Kloster Wettenhausen. Beiträge aus Geschichte und Gegenwart im Rückblick auf sein tausendjähriges Bestehen 982–1982*, Günzburger Hefte 19 (Weißenhorn: A. H. Konrad, 1983), 45–59. Dieter Bitterli, "Die emblematische Kassettendecke der Rosenburg in Stans (NW)," *Zeitschrift für Schweizerische Archäologie und Kunstgeschichte* 49 (1992): 201–220. Ojārs Spārītis, "An Iconological Interpretation of the Cycle of Emblematic Paintings in the Church at Gaiķi in Courland," in *The German-language Emblem in Its European Context: Exchange and Transmission*, ed. Anthony J. Harper and Ingrid Höpel, Glasgow Emblem Studies 5 (Glasgow: Department of French, 2000), 145–166. Ojārs Spārītis, "The Pulpit as a Medium for Educational and Political Messages in the Latvian Lutheran Church," *Emblematica. An Interdisciplinary Journal for Emblem Studies* 16 (2008): 53–75 (on the emblemata in the churches at Lestene and Burtnieki). Andreas Beck, "Mönche, Mauern und Embleme. Architekturemblematik im Kreuzgang des Klosters Wettenhausen (1680/90)," in *PerspektivWechsel oder: Die Wiederentdeckung der Philologie*, vol. 2: *Grenzgänge und Grenzüberschreitungen. Zusammenspiele von Sprache und Literatur in Mittelalter und Früher Neuzeit*, ed. Nina Bartsch and Simone Schultz-Balluff (Berlin: E. Schmidt, 2016), 289–375. Piotr Birecki, "The Lutheran Church in Rodowo as a Place of the Spiritual Meeting of Three Social Strata," *Entangled Religions* 7 (2018), 109–136.

3 Cf. note 1.

4 Cf. Birgit Emich, "Bildlichkeit und Intermedialität in der frühen Neuzeit. Eine interdisziplinäre Spurensuche," *Zeitschrift für Historische Forschung* 35 (2008): 31–56. Jörg Robert, ed., *Intermedialität in der Frühen Neuzeit. Formen, Funktionen, Konzepte*, Frühe Neuzeit 209 (Berlin and Boston: de Gruyter, 2017), Jörg Robert, *Einführung in die Intermedialität* (Darmstadt: WBG, 2014). Tobias Bulang, ed., *Johann Fischart, genannt Mentzer. Frühneuzeitliche Autorschaft im intermedialen Kontext*, Wolfenbütteler Abhandlungen zur Renaissanceforschung 37 (Wiesbaden: Harrasowitz Verlag in Kommission, 2019). Alfred Messerli and Michael Schilling, eds., *Die Intermedialität des Flugblatts in der Frühen Neuzeit* (Stuttgart: S. Hirzel, 2015). Kai Merten, *Intermediales Text-Theater. Die Bühne des Politischen und des Wissens vom Menschen bei Wordsworth und Scott*, Buchreihe der Anglia 43 (Berlin and Boston: de Gruyter, 2014).

5 Cf. Johann Anselm Steiger, *Der Orgelprospekt im Kloster Lüne als Zeugnis barock-lutherischer Bild- und Musiktheologie. Zur Intermedialität von Wort, Bild und Musik im 17. Jahrhundert* (Regensburg: Schnell & Steiner, 2015). Idem, *Bibelauslegung durch Bilder. Zur sakralen Intermedialität im 16. bis 18. Jahrhundert*, Kunst und Konfession in der Frühen Neuzeit 2 (Regensburg: Schnell & Steiner, 2018). Idem, ed., *Reformation und Medien. Zu den intermedialen Wirkungen der Reformation*, Reformation heute 4 (Leipzig: Evangelische Verlagsanstalt, 2018).

permanent-emblematic intermediality tangible at the altar to form an even more complex network of relationships. Only when one carefully takes into account these circumstances does it become tangible that the emblem cycles, which are consistently characterized by horizontal intermediality, i. e., by textual-pictorial combinations, play an essential role in achieving the goal of ensuring a spiritual diversity of media. This diversity of media addresses all the human senses (*visus, auditus, tactus, gustus, olfactus*) and affects them synaesthetically. In this way, all available means are used to ensure that in handling the means of salvation (*media salutis*), i. e., the Word of God and the sacraments, the only ultimate mediator between God and man according to 1 Tim 2:5, Christ, becomes present as the "protomedium"[6] and culmination point of vertical intermediality and, by means of this *media salutis*, mystically unites himself with the communicants, transforming them into himself and himself into them.[7]

As far as the intermediality of salvation in the christological-soteriological vertical is concerned, it is always necessary to include its bipolarity in analyses. It consists in the fact that Christ, according to contemporary reflection, acts as a protomedium in two respects within his high priestly office (*munus sacerdotale*). For the Son of God exercises this office not only in that he gives himself – in the personal union of the sacrificing high priest and of the one

sacrificed – for sinners (Heb 9:11–12) and thus saves them, but also in that after the ascension, sitting at the right hand of God, he continues to function as mediator and especially as intercessor between mankind and God the Father. For Christ permanently reminds God the Father that by means of his blood he has once and for all brought about reconciliation between God and humanity. Accordingly, it is the Son of God who keeps his Father from punishing sinful humanity by constantly reminding him that he, Christ, already had borne and atoned for all sins.

A painting in the church of Karsibór (formerly Kaseburg) on the island of the same name (Poland, West Pomeranian Voivodeship) illustrates this in a particularly impressive manner (fig. 1). Here the Son of God appears protecting the believer, who is symbolized by a kneeling female person, from the angry God, who looks down from heaven on the upper right and threatens mankind with a bundle of lightning in his right hand. The media that depicts the Son of God's protection are manifold and bring the vertical intermediality concisely in view. First, the waving red cloak offers protection from God's wrath to the person kneeling before and holding on to Christ's left ankle, thus invoking the metaphor of the protective cloak.[8] Furthermore, Christ, looking up to God

fig. 1: Painting in the church at Karsibór (Poland, West Pomeranian Voivodeship).

---

6 Philipp Stoellger, "Tod oder Leben – Unvermitteltes oder Unmittelbares? Zum Chiasmus von Theologie und Medientheorie," *Internationales Jahrbuch für Medienphilosophie* 1 (2015): 171–191, here 178.

7 Cf. Steiger (note 1), 1:153.

8 Cf. Johann Anselm Steiger, "'Nulla femina dir gleich'. Martin Luther und Maria. Zugleich ein Beitrag zur Ikonographie des Schutzmantels," in *Maria in den Konfessionen und Medien der Frühen Neuzeit*, ed. Bernhard Jahn and Claudia Schindler, Frühe Neuzeit 234 (Berlin and Boston: de Gruyter, 2020), 25 – 63.

the Father, presents him with three so-called objects of the passion (i.e., the scourge, rod, and nails) to remind him that he, Christ, has already borne God's wrath on behalf of sinful humanity and suffered his judgment as well as died on Golgotha. The painter thus depicts a synopsis of the duties of Christ's high priestly office, namely to represent actively the believing but continually sinful human being before God the Father as intercessor and to connect this with the memory of the passively (suffering and dying) achieved reconciliation of God with human beings and human beings with God (*redemptio*).

The (now fragmentary) signature attached to the painting takes the form of a short prayer in which the believer asks Christ to intercede for him with God the Father: "JEsu mit getreuer Bitt [bey] dem Vater mich vertr[itt]." ["Jesus, represent me with faithful supplication to the Father!"] The church in Karisbór presents a horizontal-intermedial thematization of the double (human and divine) mediality of the prayer, which is of central importance within the vertical intermediality since the human prayer evokes the intercession of *Christus mediator*. We must add to this a virulent idea in the early modern understanding of prayer: When believers, i.e., people endowed by the Holy Spirit, pray, they do not obey a command of God first and foremost but rather comply with his urgent request to worship him. In so doing, not only the Son of God represents them, but also the Holy Spirit "with unspeakable groanings" (Rom 8:26). With this observation, it becomes clear that prayer has a fourfold mediality. It includes the Trinitarian plurality entirely and is of fundamental importance for the vertical intermediality: When a person prays to God the Father, he responds to the request of the beloved himself; simultaneously when the believer addresses his prayer requests to the second person of the Trinity as mediator, both Jesus and the Holy Spirit in the context of their *intercessio* present these prayers to God the Father and admonish him to fulfill the requests according to his promises (*promissiones*). In this way the one praying and all the persons of the Trinity interact within the medium of prayer; in turn, the Trinity (i.e., already in themselves) is in a permanent mutual exchange that takes place from eternity (see below).

THE TRIAD OF SPIRITUAL INTERMEDIALITY, INTERTEXTUALITY, AND INTERPICTORIALITY

Against the background just sketched, it becomes clear that for the purpose of an adequate description of the spiritual-emblematic intermediality it is not sufficient to analyze the individual text-pictorial-relations. Rather, it is indispensable to include their mutual – synthetic, amplificatory, oppositive, etc. – relationality in interpretation. Hereby, we follow methodologically a hermeneutic requirement that is decisive also in the early modern theory of emblems (e.g., in that of Georg Philipp Harsdörffer [1607–1658][9]) and is thoroughly reflected, especially with respect to the so-

9 Cf. Stefan Keppler-Tasaki, "Harsdörffer, Georg Philipp," in *Frühe Neuzeit in Deutschland 1620–1720. Literaturwissenschaftliches Verfasserlexikon*, ed. Stefanie Arend, Bernhard Jahn, Jörg Robert, Robert Seidel, Johann Anselm Steiger, Stefan Tilg, Friedrich Vollhardt (Berlin and Boston: de Gruyter, 2021), 3:837–860. Rosmarie Zeller,

called emblem ensembles, i. e., the combinations and interactions of several emblems on one and the same printed page. In addition, it is also methodologically necessary to examine the emblem cycles outside the book with respect to the text-text and image-image relationships between the individual emblems, i. e., with respect to the phenomena of intertextuality (e.g., as a result of connections between keywords or of *subscriptiones* that advance one another or form a stanza when read one after the other) and interpictoriality (e.g., in the form of varying resumptions or typological connections between certain pictorial subjects). Especially in cases where individual images are not presented simply at the same level but also are arranged above and below each other, diagonal or vertical correspondences should be expected. Things are even more complex, however, when emblemata are on an altar retablo with several wings (e.g., in St. Mary's in Bad Segeberg[10]). Depending on how it is arranged, different constellations and

with them even heterogeneous expressions of image-image, text-text, and image-text-relationships can result, thus making it possible to exploit a potential that is not offered in an analogous way in book-bound emblematics. In book-bound emblematics, the production of different synoptics of individual symbols can be achieved only approximately, since it is always interrupted by the turning of pages. Conversely emblem series in the form of single-sheet prints have the advantage of being combined freely.

EMBLEMATIC ENIGMATIZING AND CONTEXTUAL DECIPHERING

In this context, consistent methodological attention should be paid to the early modern emblematic-hermeneutic principle[11] that emblems, which in themselves are already intermedial entities,[12] do not simply "illustrate" or "decorate" the texts or artefacts to which they

"Harsdörffer, Georg Philipp," in *Killy Literaturlexikon. Autoren und Werke des deutschsprachigen Kulturraumes*, ed. Wilhelm Kühlmann et al., 2nd complete, rev. ed. (Berlin and Boston, 2009), 5:20–23. Stefan Keppler-Tasaki and Ursula Kocher, eds., *Georg Philipp Harsdörffers Universalität. Beiträge zu einem uomo universale des Barock*, Frühe Neuzeit 158 (Berlin and Boston: de Gruyter, 2011).

10 Cf. Steiger (note 1), 1:39–158.

11 Cf. [Georg Philipp Harsdörffer,] *Neue Zugabe: Bestehend in C. Sinnbildern Welche Auf Fahnen/ Schaupfenninge/ in Stammbüchern/ Tappeten/ Becher/ Gläser/ Flaschen/ Schalen/ Teller/ zu trauer und Freudengedichten/ wie auch zu andrer Zierlichkeit/ nach Belieben/ gebrauchet werden können. Aus Alciato, Jovio, Ruscelli, Bargagli, Capacio, Sambucco, Burgundia, Pallavicino, Camillo Camilli, Petra-Sancta, Masen und andern gesamlet/ Wie auch mit vielen neuen Erfindungen die zwey- drey- vier- fünff- und sechsständig Sinnbilder betreffend/ und Einer Vorrede*

von den Lehrsätzen dieser Kunst vermehret (Hamburg: J. Naumann, 1656), in [idem,] *Der Grosse Schau-Platz jämmerlicher Mordgeschichte. Bestehend in CC. traurigen Begebenheiten Mit vielen merkwürdigen Erzehlungen/ neu üblichen Gedichten/ Lehrreichen Sprüchen/ scharffsinnigen/ artigen/ Schertzfragen und Antworten/ etc. Verdolmetscht und mit einem Bericht von den Sinnbildern wie auch hundert Exempeln derselben als einer neuen Zugabe/ auß den berühmsten [sic!] Autoribus [...]. Zum drittenmahl gedruckt*, BSB München P. o. germ. 577 f (Hamburg: J. Naumann, 1656), here the "Vorrede. Bestehend in 50. Lehrsätzen/ von der Sinnbild-Kunst.," esp. 4–5 (2nd pagination).

12 Cf. Stefanie Arend, "Vorüberlegungen zum Entwurf einer intermedialen Rhetorik anhand von emblematischen Figurationen in der Frühen Neuzeit," in *Intermedialität in der Frühen Neuzeit. Formen, Funktionen, Konzepte*, ed. Jörg Robert, Frühe Neuzeit 209 (Berlin and Boston: de Gruyter, 2017), 287–305.

are attached, or merely duplicate or repeat certain firmly established or even self-evident statements. Rather, by means of text-image combinations, which Matthias Holtzwart (ca. 1540 – before 1579) tried to conceptualize as "Picta Poesis" or "Gemälpoesy,"[13] emblems have a *prima vista* surprising, sometimes strange, or even hermeneutic quality, i. e., a fact to be deciphered and translated[14] (not infrequently laboriously) in the synopsis of images and short texts and to generate semantic added values. As is well know, it would be an inappropriate oversimplification to think that the short texts decode the enigmatic *picturae* entirely. Therefore, for example, Harsdörffer says that "a symbol" has "eine verborgne […] Bedeutung" ["a hidden meaning"] which is "[durch] die Beyschrift angedeute[t]" ["insinuated by the inscription"].[15] Rather, there always remains (at least) an enigmatic remainder with which the recipients and their erudite interpretive competence must come to terms with divinatorially. Furthermore, the short texts themselves can have

a function constituting the *picturae*, whereas the *picturae* can also contribute to deciphering themselves, especially through inter-pictorial relations offered in the image.[16] This is surprisingly often the case in Gabriel Rollenhagen's *Nucleus Emblematum* (1583 – 1619),[17] for example, in the emblem (fig. 2) representing the pelican bringing its dead young to life with the help of its blood. Motto and *subscriptio* interpret the *pictura* not spiritually but ethically-politically and refer it – as is already present in the impression of King Alfonso I of Naples (1396 – 1458)[18] – to the good prince who is willing to lay down his life for the preservation of the law and his subjects. The ethical-political and at the same time spiritual double coding of the pelican motif is, however, taken into account by the fact that the scene in the foreground is explained in an inter-pictorial way in the background on the left. Here one looks at Christ crucified and his blood shed, as well as at people who collect this *medium salutis* in communion cups in order to consume it.[19]

13 Achim Aurnhammer and Nicolas Detering, *Deutsche Literatur der Frühen Neuzeit* (Stuttgart: UTB, 2019), 112. On Holtzwart, cf. Dietmar Peil, "Holtzwart, Mathias," in *Frühe Neuzeit in Deutschland 1520 – 1620. Literaturwissenschaftliches Verfasserlexikon*, ed. Wilhelm Kühlmann, Jan-Dirk Müller, Michael Schilling, Johann Anselm Steiger, Friedrich Vollhardt (Berlin and Boston: de Gruyter, 2014) 3:386 – 393.

14 Cf., e.g., Albrecht Schöne, "Hohbergs Psalter-Embleme," *Deutsche Vierteljahrsschrift für Literaturwissenschaft und Geistesgeschichte* 44 (1970): 655 – 669, esp. 657 – 658. Idem, *Emblematik und Drama im Zeitalter des Barock*, 3rd ed. (München: Beck, 1993), 38 – 39, *passim*.

15 Georg Philipp Harsdörffer, *Kunstverständiger Discurs, von der edlen Mahlerey. Nürnberg 1652*, ed. Michael Thimann (Heidelberg: Manutius, 2008), 13.

16 Cf. Schöne, *Emblematik und Drama* (note 14), 20 – 21.

17 Cf. Sabine Mödersheim, "Rollenhagen, Gabriel," in *Frühe Neuzeit in Deutschland 1520 – 1620. Literaturwissenschaftliches Verfasserlexikon*, ed. Wilhelm Kühlmann, Jan-Dirk Müller, Michael Schilling, Johann Anselm Steiger, Friedrich Vollhardt (Berlin and Boston: de Gruyter, 2016), 5:335 – 339.

18 Cf. Steiger, Schilling, Arend, *Sinnbilder im Sakralraum* (note 2), 250.

19 Cf. Gabriel Rollenhagen, *Sinn-Bilder. Ein Tugendspiegel*, revised with an afterword and edited by Carsten-Peter Warncke (Dortmund: Harenberg, 1983), 253. On this, cf. Dietmar Peil, "Das Emblem als Mittel symbolischer Kommunikation in der Frühen Neuzeit," in *The Mediation of Symbol in Late Medieval and Early Modern Times. Medien der Symbolik in Spätmittelalter und Früher Neuzeit*, ed. Rudolf Suntrup, Jan R. Veenstra, Anne Bollmann, Medieval to Early Modern Culture 5 (Frankfurt a. M. et al.: P. Lang, 2005), 57 – 81, here 61.

Another relevant example in this regard is in the work of Catharina Regina von Greiffenberg (1633–1694):[20] The emblem etching (fig. 3) visualizes the sunflower aligned with Christ as the Sun of Righteousness (Mal 3:20). The Son of God, whose head is surrounded by the sun, is set in the upper left of the image – in a heavenly scene in which he receives a believing soul accompanied by angels, carrying a chalice and a wafer (as the usual epithets of *fides*). The resulting message is that in their earthly life believers should permanently align themselves with the Son of God, like the sunflower with the sun, to be united one day with the Sun of Righteousness in heaven. The inter-pictoriality described here is strengthened

20 Cf. Hartmut Laufhütte and Ralf Schuster, "Greiffenberg, Catharina Regina von," in *Frühe Neuzeit in Deutschland 1620–1720. Literaturwissenschaftliches Verfasserlexikon*, ed. Stefanie Arend, Bernhard Jahn, Jörg Robert, Robert Seidel, Johann Anselm Steiger, Stefan Tilg, Friedrich Vollhardt (Berlin and Boston: de Gruyter, 2021), 3:524–535.

fig. 3: Catharina Regina von Greiffenberg, *Der Allerheiligsten Menschwerdung/ Geburt und Jugend JEsu Christi/ Zwölf Andächtige Betrachtungen:* […], BSB München Rar. 4284 (Nürnberg: J. Hofmann 1678), beside p. 609.

by the fact that the wafer carried along by the pious soul functions as an image bearer (and thus as a further image in an image). For the wafer bears the sign of the cross, which calls to memory the place where the now heavenly Christ formerly acquired salvation on earth. Here, too, the inter-pictorial correspondences tangible in the *pictura* itself contribute decisively to the interpretation of the emblem and show that the believing soul, which in its earthly life used the elements of the Lord's Supper, bread and wine, as media of an encounter with the (hidden) real Christ present in them, is taken up after its death into the bodily encounter with Christ face to face.

Emblems confront their readers or viewers with the task of tracking down heterogenous, namely intermedial, inter-pictorial, and intertextual relations and unraveling them in a concentrated, lingering, synaesthetic, and meditative-ruminative[21] way – whether as individuals placed on their own or in dialogical discourse (see below). However, this is often complicated by the fact that the signs within the emblem-*picturae* can be coded doubly or even several times. This is the case not only with the pelican but also, for example, with the diamond, which, in addition to signifying the hardening or hardness of heart of sinful man, can also signify the purity of the Virgin Mary or the Son of God.[22] This double or multiple coding results in a twofold ambiguity or a multitude of ambiguities that must be solved in each specific case by intermedial interpretation. This, however, can be complicated by the fact that, according to Harsdörffer, even the inscriptions of an emblem sometimes "einen doppelten Verstand haben" ["have a double meaning"],[23] so that in certain cases one can be dealing with intermedial syntheses of images *and* texts with a double meaning or a multitude of meanings. According to Harsdörffer, even the phenomenon of ambiguity can be grasped emblematically, namely in the form of the echo,[24] which

---

21 On this, cf. Seraina Plotke, "Frömmigkeit als synästhetische Erfahrung. Emblematik und visuelle Poesie in der Andachts- und Gebetsliteratur der Frühen Neuzeit," in *Das Gebet in den Konfessionen und Medien der Frühen Neuzeit*, ed. Johann Anselm Steiger, Theologie – Kultur – Hermeneutik 25 (Leipzig: Evangelische Verlagsanstalt, 2018), 161–175, esp. 165–167.

22 Cf. Steiger (note 1), 8:113–118.

23 Cf. Georg Philipp Harsdörffer, *DELITIAE MATHEMATICAE ET PHYSICAE Der Mathematischen und Philosophischen Erquickstunden Zweyter Theil: Bestehend in Fünffhundert nutzlichen und lustigen Kunstfragen/ nachsinnigen Aufgaben/ und deroselben grundrichtigen Erklärungen/ Auß Athanasio Kirchero, Petro Bettino, Marino Mersennio, Renato des Cartes, Orontio Fineo, Marino Gethaldo, Cornelio Drebbelio, Alexandro Tassoni, Sanctorio Sanctorii, Marco Marci, und vielen andern Mathematicis und Physicis zusammen getragen [...]*, Staatliche Bibliothek Regensburg 999/Philos. 2181[2]), (Nürnberg: J. Dümler, 1651), 4r.

24 Cf. Georg Philipp Harsdörffer, *Ars Apophthegmatica, Das ist: Kunstquellen Denckwürdiger Lehrsprüche und Ergötzlicher Hofreden; Wie solche Nachsinnig zu suchen/ erfreulich zu finden/ anständig zugebrauchen und schicklich zu beantworten: in Drey Tausend Exempeln/ aus Hebräischen/ Syrischen/ Arabischen/ Persischen/ Griechischen/ Lateinischen/ Spanischen/ Jtalianischen/ Frantzösischen/ Engländischen/ Nieder- und Hochteutschen Scribenten/ angewiesen/ und mit Dreysig Schertz-Schreiben/ als einer besondern Beylage vermehret [...]*, BSB München Res/L.eleg.m. 591-1 (Nürnberg: W. Endter d. J., J. A. Endter, 1655), 14. Cf. Ferdinand van Ingen, *Echo im 17. Jahrhundert. Ein literarisch-musikalisches Phänomen in der Frühen Neuzeit*, Koninklijke Nederlandse Akademie van Wetenschappen, Mededelingen van de Afdeling Letterkunde, Nieuwe Reeks 65/2 (Amsterdam: Koninklijke Nederlandse Akademie van Wetenschappen, 2002).

gives the caller an answer that sounds similar to the call, and yet goes far beyond it.

Certainly, disambiguities arise in the interpretive process of an emblem's significance, which is initiated mostly by *subscriptio* accompanying the emblem, if one is present. This is the case, for example, when ethical instruction for action is formulated or a doctrine of faith is in focus. However, such disambiguities continuously exist in the intermedial context of their *picturae* (and possibly their "epigraphs") with which they are connected. At the end the *picturae* and their short texts remain ambiguous, a fact that interpretation cannot fully eliminate. Moreover, such ambiguous spiritual emblems relate to the reality of life and faith of human beings, who likewise are and remain enigmas as long as, according to Col 3:3, their "Leben verborgen [ist] mit Christo in Gott" ["life is hidden with Christ in God"] (see below). In this respect, it is hardly surprising that it was not emblematics insisting on a plurality of levels of meaning that failed against mentalities of the Enlightenment period, such as neology which demanded rational unambiguity. On the contrary, the latter were overtaxed to adapt adequately the *eruditio* compressed in the highest density in emblematics, together with its roots reaching back into (Christian and pagan) antiquity. An anti-emblematic iconoclasm was obvious in light of this excessive demand, but it did not solve the self-imposed problem.

To summarize what has been said above methodologically, different media relations and synergies must be decoded in the course of decoding emblemata:

- first, the connection between emblem-*pictura* and the respective short texts (*subscriptio, inscriptio, superscriptio*), thus the signs offered in the picture (*signa*) and the things designated or indicated in the short texts (*res significatae*),[25]
- second, the possibly existent inter-pictorial references in the emblem-*pictura* itself and the inner-pictorial interpretive potentials hidden in them,
- third, the intertextual references offered in the emblem, which result from the comparative reading of the short texts and
- fourth, the likewise enigmatic coherence between the respective emblem as a whole and its literary micro- and macro-context or its embedding outside the book – contexts that regularly opens up additional intermedial, inter-pictorial, and intertextual dimensions.

It is obvious that such an intermedial interplay of pictorial and textual forms of expression and their mutual reflexivity, which aims at playfully demonstrating the transparency of everything representational for the spiritual,[26] virtually suggests a playful form of reception – and this not only on the part of individual recipients, i. e., individuals who remain "alone" in secluded

---

25 Cf. Harsdörffer, *Neue Zugabe* (note 11), 5. On this, cf. (with reference especially to the relevant work of Carsten-Peter Warncke) Ulrich Heinen, "Argument – Kunst – Affekt. Bildverständnisse einer Kunstgeschichte der Frühen Neuzeit," in *Die Frühe Neuzeit als Epoche*, ed. Helmut Neuhaus, Historische Zeitschrift, Beihefte N. F. 49 (München: Oldenbourg, 2009), 165–234, here 208.

26 Cf. Ferdinand van Ingen, *Wort, Zeichen, Bild und die Kultur des reformatorischen Wissens. Zu Fragen der Emblematik und Metaphorik im 17. Jahrhundert* (Passau: Ralf Schuster Verlag, 2017), 49–50. See further Warncke, "Allegorese als Gesellschaftsspiel" (note 2).

devotion, but also in convivial conversation, which retraces, deepens, and enriches the relationships in interpersonal communication that are inherent in the emblems themselves (and also take place between them). The form of reception and communication suggested by cycles of emblems in sacred spaces is therefore (similar to what has recently been worked out for early modern painting[27]) not exclusively based on individualized meditation or monologic preaching, but on discursive sociality and communicative exchange.[28] The same is true for the literary genre of baroque conversation games that developed after Giovanni Boccaccio's (1313–1375) *Decamerone*[29] – for example, in the form of Harsdörffer's *Frauenzimmer Gesprächspiele*[30] or Johann Rist's (1607–1667) *Monatsgespräche*,[31] but also in the form of the specifically spiritual conversation game

penned by Sigmund von Birken (1626–1681)[32] with the title *Gottselige Gespräch-Lust*.[33] It is no coincidence that emblematic (or, in Birken's case, spiritual-emblematic) motifs play a central role in these dialogical texts and that they can be used for communal, mutual entertainment or edification. In the texts mentioned, emblems are often the objects of conversational discussion. However, the literary form of the individual speech processes of the interlocutors also are very often characterized by emblematic language and imagery. For example, even the most banal everyday acts, such as personal hygiene, are investigated for their symbolic valence.[34] In any case, it is clear that the synergy of media, as is present in emblemata, evokes and requires the synergy of interpreters in communication – and this is not only true for the early modern period, but to a greater

27 Cf. Wolfgang Brassat, *Das Bild als Gesprächsprogramm. Selbstreflexive Malerei und ihr kommunikativer Gebrauch in der Frühen Neuzeit* (Berlin and Boston: de Gruyter, 2021).

28 This aspect could be used to expand the set of varieties of sociability that Walter Sparn precisely describes: cf. Walter Sparn, "Christ-löbliche Fröhlichkeit. Naturrechtliche und offenbarungstheologische Legitimationen der Geselligkeit in der Frühen Neuzeit," in idem, *Frömmigkeit, Bildung, Kultur. Theologische Aufsätze I: Lutherische Orthodoxie und christliche Aufklärung in der frühen Neuzeit*, Marburger Theologische Studien 103 (Leipzig: Evangelische Verlagsanstalt, 2012), 113–134.

29 Cf. Rosmarie Zeller, "Das Gespräch als Medium der Wissensvermittlung," in *Natur – Religion – Medien. Transformationen frühneuzeitlichen Wissens*, ed. Thorsten Burkard, Diskursivierung von Wissen in der Frühen Neuzeit 2 (Berlin: Akademie Verlag, 2013), 229–247. See further Thomas Fries and Klaus Weimar, "Dialog 2," *Reallexikon der Deutschen Literaturwissenschaft* 1 (1997): 354–356.

30 Mara R. Wade, "From Reading to Writing: Women Authors and Book Collectors at the Wolfenbüttel Court – A Case Study of Georg Philipp Harsdörffer's

'Frauenzimmer Gesprächspiele,'" *German Life and Letters* 67 (2014): 181–195.

31 Cf. Nicola Kaminski, "'Monatliche Unterredungen, ist ein Journal'. Rists 'Jänners'- bis 'Brachmonats'-Unterredungen im Horizont von Zeitschriften- und Fortsetzungsliteratur," in *Johann Rist (1607–1667). Profil und Netzwerke eines Pastors, Dichters und Gelehrten*, ed. Johann Anselm Steiger and Bernhard Jahn, Frühe Neuzeit 195 (Berlin and Boston: de Gruyter, 2015), 587–610 as well as Rosmarie Zeller, "Sinnkünste. Sinnbilder und Gemälde in Harsdörffers 'Frauenzimmer Gesprächspielen,'" in *Georg Philipp Harsdörffer und die Künste*, ed. Doris Gerstl, Schriftenreihe der Akademie der Bildenden Künste in Nürnberg 10 (Nürnberg: H. Carl, 2005), 215–229.

32 Cf. Johann Anselm Steiger, "(Bild-)Rhetorik des Gesprächs. Zur Emblematik des Alltags in Sigmund von Birkens 'Gottseeliger Gespräch-Lust,'" *Rhetorik. Ein internationales Jahrbuch* 34 (2015): 79–94.

33 Cf. Sigmund von Birken, *Erbauungsschrifttum*. 2 Parts, ed. Johann Anselm Steiger, Thomas Illg, Ralf Schuster, Sigmund von Birken, Werke und Korrespondenz 8 = Neudrucke Deutscher Literaturwerke NF 79–80 (Berlin and Boston: de Gruyter, 2014), 183–422.

34 Cf. Steiger, "(Bild-)Rhetorik" (note 32).

extent also today. This is shown simply by the fact that adequate research of emblematics as well as of early modern intermediality – and not least of spirituality – can succeed only in a synergic-interdisciplinary manner.

Remarkably, the emblem-hermeneutical problem of the interplay between enigmatization and de-enigmatization is expressed in a specific and quite complex way at the pulpit of the church at Vedersø (Denmark, Central Jutland; see fig. 4). On the balustrade of the pulpit, there are four emblematic paintings that speak heterogeneously to the task of the preacher or the office of preaching. Above the emblemata is a Greek inscription running around the pulpit that reproduces the text of 1 Cor 14:11 – a verse in which the apostle Paul speaks of the necessity of translating and interpreting the tongues (*glossolalia*) of spiritually gifted members of the Corinthian congregation. The inscription reads: ἐὰν οὖν μὴ εἰδῶ τὴν δύναμιν τῆς φωνῆς, ἔσωμαι τω [correct: ἔσομαι τῷ] λαλοῦντι βάρβαρος καὶ ὁ λαλῶν, ἐν ἐμοι [correct: ἐμοὶ] βάρβαρος. Luther translated the verse as follows: "So ich nun nicht weiß der Stimme Deutung, werde ich undeutsch [= unverständlich] sein dem, der da redet, und der da redet, wird mir undeutsch sein" ["Therefore, if I do not know the meaning of the voice, I will be un-German [= incomprehensible] to the one who speaks, and he who speaks will be un-German to me"]. According to Paul, *glossolalia*, which is at first unintelligible to the fellow Christians, is permissible as long as those who speak in tongues are careful to "pray" not only "with the spirit" but also "with understanding" (1 Cor 14:15), i. e., not to leave the speech which cannot be understood by others but instead to decipher it and thus make it communicable and understandable. In a marginal note, Luther extrapolates from this, i. e., referring to any speech-*actus*, and says: "Mit dem Sinn reden ist eben so viel als auslegen und den Sinn den anderen verklären [= erklären]. Aber im Geist reden ist den Sinn selbst verstehen und nicht auslegen." ["To speak according to sense is just as much as to interpret and to explain the sense to the others. But to speak in the spirit is to understand the sense itself and not to interpret it."] Here, then, we are concerned with granting participation made possible by the hermeneutical processes of unraveling, interpretation, and translation. In this sense, according to Matthias Flacius Illyricus (1520–1575),[35] 1 Cor 14 is a key New Testament text in terms of determining what *interpretatio* is, as he unfolds in his *Clavis scripturae sacrae*. According to this, interpretation (1) simply has to do with translation from one language to another, (2) with the explanation of difficult, thus dark (not least prophetic) texts of Holy Scripture, (3) with the interpretation of dreams and visions, and finally (4) with the task of clearly expressing the contents, i. e., of teaching ("clare dicere, aut docere"[36]).

fig. 4: Pulpit in the church at Vedersø (Denmark, Central Jutland).

35 Cf. Norbert Kössinger and Johann Anselm Steiger, "Flacius Illyricus, Matthias," in *Frühe Neuzeit in Deutschland 1520–1620. Literaturwissenschaftliches Verfasserlexikon*, ed. Wilhelm Kühlmann, Jan-Dirk Müller, Michael Schilling, Johann Anselm Steiger, Friedrich Vollhardt (Berlin and Boston: de Gruyter, 2012), 2:383–399.

36 Matthias Flacius Illyricus, *CLAVIS SCRIPTVRAE S. seu de Sermone Sacrarum literarum [...] PARS PRIMA: IN QVA SINGVLARVM VOCVM, ATQVE*

With regard to the inscription and the pictorial program of the pulpit in the church at Vedersø, a complex constellation now arises. First, the Greek inscription quoting 1 Cor 14:11 is already the subject of translation and interpretation with respect to the members of the congregation who do not speak Greek. Second, this verse marks one of the central official duties of pastors acting within the pulpit. This task consists in translating and interpreting not only the verse in question but also the biblical texts to be preached, and in making them comprehensible and usable according to the homiletical rules of the art. Third, the text of 1 Cor 14:11, which itself requires decoding, provides a methodological guideline for dealing with the emblemata found in the pulpit (and elsewhere). They need to be deciphered – and this must be done in the awareness that these emblemata remain enigmatic in spite of the interpretations given them and therefore are similar to the biblical texts which must be preached anew each time. For according to the early modern view, the enigmaticity by no means determines only the emblemata, but is a characteristic of God's revelation as a whole until Judgment Day. Therefore, Luther, for example, emphasizes that the *verbum Dei* attested in the Holy Scriptures – irrespective of its *claritas* – is at the same time fundamentally characterized by mysteriousness, because up until the final revelation of God on Judgment Day everything in the word of God ultimately is concealed and hidden.[37] Therefore, the unceasing discovery and uncovering of the word of God is the permanent task of the (multimedial) sermon. According to Luther, the same applies to the enigmatic manifestation of God through and in the God-man Jesus Christ, who appears to the rational gaze, i. e., not yet illuminated by faith, to be a mere man. The same applies to the concealment of Christ's flesh and blood in the elements of the Lord's Supper, the bread and wine,[38] as well as to the proclamation of the Son of God, which, according to Matt 13:34–35, made extensive use of parables, that is, of riddles ("retzlin seu aenigmata"[39]), which necessarily require decoding and interpretation. In addition, it would be a misunderstanding to think that, according to Luther, the hidden God (*Deus absconditus*) alone is the first person of the trinity who remains invisible, while the revealed God (*Deus revelatus*) simply is to be equated with Christ. According to Luther, God's revelation in his Son is characterized by a maximum of abscondity and angularity, especially with regard to the "precise hiddenness of God"[40] in the suffering and dying crucified one.[41] In this respect, the *Deus relevatus* in the form of the *Christus absconditus* is the special

---

locutionum S. Scripturae usus ac ratio Alphabetico ordine explicatur. [...], BSB München 2 Exeg. 220-1/2 (Basel: J. Oporinus, 1567), 619–620, citation p. 620.

37 Cf. Martin Luther, *Werke. Kritische Gesamtausgabe*, 73 vols., Weimar edition 1883–2009 (henceforth cited Luther, WA according to volume, pages, and lines), here Luther, WA 13.659.12–14: "[...] adhuc omnia tantum in verbo latent, est adhuc regnum fidei, sunt omnia in aenigmate, ut inquit Paulus, donec veniat dies, quo revelentur omnia de facie ad faciem."

38 Cf. Luher, WA 18.143.9–10.

39 Luther, WA 38.565.34–35.

40 Cf. here Heinrich Assel, *Elementare Christologie*, vol. 3: *Inkarnation des Menschen und Menschwerdung Gottes* (Gütersloh: Gütersloher Verlagshaus, 2020), 241.

41 Cf. Luther, WA 12.511.1–17. On this matter, cf. Johann Anselm Steiger and Heinrich Assel, "Hiddenness of God. IV. Christianity. B. Modern Europe and America," in *Encyclopedia of the Bible and Its Reception* (Berlin and Boston: de Gruyter, 2015), 11:1025–1031.

focus of Luther's theology, since "Christus [= Christi] Reich und Macht ist unter dem Kreuz verborgen" ["Christ's kingdom and power are hidden under the cross"], which necessitates the medial engagement with this very facticity in "Predigen, Lehren und Bekennen" ["preaching, teaching, and confessing."][42]

It is no different with the Holy Spirit, who appears in the form of a dove, thus in a medium (*quodam medio*), and is perceived through a cover (*per involucrum*) as a riddle ("enigma") and makes his message audible with a human voice (*voce humana*[43]). But also Christians living in the earthly context, to whom justification and eternal beatitude are already promised for the sake of their faith, exist – according to Luther – in a body that is still subject to all kinds of evils, and are thereby paradoxically preserved toward eternal life as in a hidden riddle ("ceu in abscondito aenigmate"[44]). Here, the reformer implicitly refers to Col 3:3, which speaks of the believer's "life" being "hidden with Christ in God." Luther interprets this key text elsewhere to the effect that believing and justified Christians, as far as their external existence is concerned ("according to the flesh"), are "still in the grave with Christ" until Judgment Day,

> ob wir wohl Vergebung der Sünden haben, Gottes Kinder und selig sind, doch dasselbe noch nicht vor unsern und der Welt Augen und Sinnen ist, sondern in Christo durch den Glauben verborgen und zugedeckt bis an den Jüngsten Tag. Denn es scheinet und fühlet sich kein' solche Gerechtigkeit, Hei-

ligkeit, Leben und Seligkeit, wie doch das Wort sagt und der Glaube fassen muß. Daher auch St. Paulus Kolosser 3:3 – 4 spricht […]: "Euer Leben ist verborgen mit Christo in Gott, wenn aber Christus, euer Leben, sich offenbaret, so werdet auch ihr offenbar werden mit ihm in der Herrlichkeit."[45] [even though we have forgiveness of sins, are God's children, and are blessed, nevertheless this is not yet before our and the world's eyes and senses, but is hidden and covered up in Christ through faith until the last day. For no such righteousness, holiness, life, and blessedness appears or feels as the word says and faith must grasp. Therefore, even St. Paul says in Col 3:3 – 4: "Your life is hidden with Christ in God, but when Christ, your life, is revealed, then you also will be revealed with him in glory."]

From this, however, the following results: First, at least in this life, enigmatization determines every variety of vertical and horizontal mediality and intermediality, which can be deciphered only partially and tentatively. However, this did not result in resignation in the early modern period. On the contrary, great efforts were made to contribute to deciphering the mysteries of the triune God and his message by using all available media. Second, in any act of deciphering the word of God – of course also when presented in emblematic media – by one who strives to find the solution to the riddle, it must be kept in mind always that he himself is a riddle.

---

42 Luther, WA 38.67.7 – 8.
43 Luther, WA 39/I.216.31 – 32; 217.24.
44 Luther, WA 25.387.8.
45 Luther, WA 22.96.8 – 17.

DE-ENIGMATIZING OF EMBLEMATA AS PROLEPSIS OF ESCHATOLOGICAL DECIPHERING

The fact that emblemata are permanently enigmatic and the resulting necessity that the interpreter, who himself is an enigma, must decipher them ever anew, is not only relevant to the appreciation and use of the interrelated media of text and image, but also to the theological criticism of media reflected here. This takes into account the fact that no available medium and no variety of intermediality – not even the emblematic one – will ever be able to represent fully what is conveyed as long as the eschatological realization of the *beata visio a facie ad faciem* (1 Cor 13:12) – and thus the recovery of the original encounter with God lost by the fall (*lapsus*) of the arch-parents – is still pending. Spiritual mediality must come to terms with this eschatological reservation, which must always be reflected in its protological-hamartiological context, and in this respect always and necessarily includes skepticism with respect to the media and criticism of the media. For the representation of the divine in the horizontal media is understood as proleptic, i.e., provisional. This is due, among other things, to the fact that the *Christus praesens* has largely eluded empirical perception since the ascension and until Judgment Day, which is why the spiritual media (the sacraments, the *verbum Dei*, etc.) have particularly important and at the same time provisional functions in the tension between withdrawal and presence.

Spiritual intermediality aims (taking this into account) nevertheless and paradoxically so at giving the earthly presence of God, which has become tangible in the incarnation, maximum tangibility and at the same time attempts to deal with the insufficiency of horizontal intermediality. Such striving for medial representation of the medially (still) incompletely perceptible is a concretion of the certainty that the final evidence and all-encompassing unraveling according to 1 Cor 13:12 will be attained only in the *visio beatifica* on Judgment Day, at the time, therefore, when vertical and horizonal mediality collapse into one. It goes without saying that in view of this eschatological-hermeneutical process of complete de-enigmatization still to come, the unraveling of emblemata has a proleptic, so to speak prelude-like function. This is of the greatest relevance, since the deciphering of spiritual emblemata makes possible preceding exercises in the practice of the vision of God face-to-face in the heavenly home. This is a vision that will no longer be a "Spiegel-Schau" ["mirror vision"] but a "Selbst-Schau" ["essential vision"], "da wir ihn [= Christus] nicht mehr abstractive, sondern intuitive vom Angesicht zu Angesicht sehen werden"[46] ["since we will no longer see him [Christ] abstractly but intuitively, face-to-

---

46 Andreas Christoph Schubart, *Evangelischer Lehr-Tempel/ Jn welchem Auß allen Sonn- und Fest-Tags Evangelien Die Geistliche Sehe-Kunst/ Die Evangel. GOttes-Lehre/ Die allerbesten Kern-Sprüche/ Die sonderbarn Geheimnüß-Bilder/ Die Biblische Mahler-Kunst/ Die Evang. Hertzens-Eröffnung/ Die Schatz-Kammer GOttes/ Die nöthige Seelen-Rettung/ Das innerl. Gewissens-Gerichte/ Der richtige Him-mels-Weg/ Die Christliche Höllen-Flucht/ Der Schauplatz des neuen Menschen/ Und die Geistliche Fruchtbringende Gesellschafft/ Nebenst der Christlichen Weisheit-Schule/ auß den gewöhnlichen Sonn- und Fest-TagsEpisteln/ Meistens unter lauter Special-Thematibus auff vorhergehende Vorbereitungen und Eingänge betrachtet werden/ Also/ daß in Vierzehen Lehr-Arthen Uber 900. kürtzlich zusammen gezogene*

face"], as the Lutheran pastor Pastor Andreas Christoph Schubart (1629–1689), who served in Halle an der Saale, put it, in reference to 1 John 3:2: "We are now children of God; and it has not yet appeared what we will be. But we know, when it does appear, that we will be like him, for we will see him as he is."

This, however, means: Only in the no longer mirrored and inverted, but intuitive-essential vision of Christ in eternal life, by this very vision the abscondity and the enigmaticity of man, who has already become new through faith, will be removed and his *regeneratio* will be completed in full. The transition into this new status will, of course, be connected with a change of medium. Luther makes this clear when he generates an eschatological chiasm from the Pauline statement "we walk by faith and not by sight" (2 Cor 5:7), according to which here faith (*fides*) and not sight is the medium of God's encounter, whereas in the eternal kingdom of heaven it will conversely not be faith but sight: "Istud regnum coelorum est fidei, tum visionis, Schauens. Hic oportet credamus, non videmus, sed tum videbimus, non credemus."[47] To put it more pointedly, the principle *sola fide* has its validity until Judgment Day, when *visio* takes the place of faith.

However, this very reflection on the prospect of the eschatological-intuitive vision *without* faith is the condition of the possibility for the approximation of the vision of faith in this life. This faith has the ability to detect the spiritual transparency of the occlusions and enigmata, that is, to decipher counterfactually the glory (δόξα) of the Lord (John 1:14) under the opposite or counter-image of the sin-bearing Lamb of God to whom John the Baptist pointed (John 1:29, 36). It is faith that affects inner enlightenment (*collustratio interna*). This enables him to decipher the texts of the Holy Scripture (*liber scripturae*) – even those that use figurative-parabolic language – as well as the book of nature (*liber naturae*) as a spiritual codex and thesaurus of the masks (*larvae*) of God[48] according to faith (*per analogiam fidei*). Emblem artists borrow innumerable pictorial motifs precisely from this book of nature and enrich this reservoir with *picturae* that represent man-made artefacts and point to the spiritual significance embedded in them. And it is precisely this faith that the believer, in the face of the maltreated Christ, crowned with thorns and dead, paradoxically sees the clarity of God – not a partial or only a diminished reflection of it, but "des ganzen Wesens Glanz"[49] ["the entire splendor of [divine] essence"] – in its concealment. This is exactly what is depicted in numerous pictorial representations of Golgotha that present the crucified one in largely shadowed scenery and simultaneously with a luminous halo of rays surrounding his inclined head. Here it becomes iconographically comprehensible what the apostle Paul

---

Predigten zu befinden sind/ Wobey ein ANHANG von sechs Predigten/ als: Eine Gast- Prob- zwey Anzugs- Neue-Jahrs- und Feuer-Predigt/ Niemand anders als neu-angehenden Predigern Zu einiger Anleitung auff vielfältiges Begehren durch öffentlichen Druck eröffnet [...], HAB Wolfenbüttel 158.7 Theol. (Halle/ Leipzig: S. J. Hübner 1672), 25.

47 Luther, WA 49.574.8–10.
48 Cf. Luther, WA 40/I.174.13–14: "Universa autem creatura est facies et larva Dei." Cf. further, e.g., WA 17/ II.192.28–29.
49 Luther, WA 50.276.24.

means when he says, "For God, who caused the light to shine out of darkness, has given a bright light shining in our hearts, that through us might come the illumination of the knowledge of the glory of God in the face of Jesus Christ" (2 Cor 4:6).

The *ars emblematica* operates precisely within this tension between *absconditas* and *revelatio*, between *obscuritas* and *claritas*, between enigma and unraveling or darkness and clarity and pursues a complex hermeneutic conception that is expressed particularly succinctly in the title copperplate of the *Lux Evangelica* by the Jesuit Heinrich Engelgrave (1610–1670) (fig. 5). Here, in the medium of a copperplate engraving, which can be described as emblematic not only as a whole but also in its individual parts, the program of spiritual symbolic art is presented. The title of the work, which announces the presentation of the *Lux Evangelica* (the evangelical light) under the curtain (*sub velum*) of holy emblems, is sensibly noted on a curtain. This is stretched by putti, each carrying an emblem, obscuring the view of Holy Scripture and three of the four evangelists, symbolized by a young woman and by a lion, a bull, and an eagle, from the potential viewer who stands directly in front of the curtain. That the emblems are intended to be deciphered, such that the *velum* becomes transparent and thus the light emanating from the open Holy Scripture becomes perceptible, is cleverly made visible by the engraved title on copperplate through the arrangement of the pictorial composition. The viewer is placed in such a way that he does not look at the scene from the front but from the side, looks past the concealing curtain, and sees the symbols of the evangelists that are revealed in their hiddenness, as well as the open Holy Scripture, from

which rays emanate. These rays correspond to the rays of light visible in the *picturae* of the four emblem medallions that the putti carry. Thus it is made clear that it is about the horizontal-intermedial reciprocity of the illumination of the Gospels by the emblemata and vice versa of the emblemata by the Gospel texts – with the help of the divine light, which is vertically-intermedially mediated by the Holy Spirit, who floats down from heaven in the form of a dove at the top left and provides the medium, without which the whole scenery would be in darkness and invisible: the divine light.

All four emblems deal with the tense bipolarities of concealment and disclosure, invisibility and visibility, and darkness and light, with reference to ancient pagan texts. What is presented on this title copperplate could be called meta-emblematics, for it is nothing other than a fourfold emblematic self-reflection of the *ars emblematica* and the dialectic specific to it. The symbol on the upper left (fig. 6) represents a sun and a rainbow; the motto accompanying the image reads "Mille colores" ("a thousand colors"), referring to *Metamorphoses* Book 6 (6.65–66) where Ovid (43–17 BCE) states that the rainbow has a thousand visible colors. Invisible to the observer, however, is the "transitus," that is, the transition of one color into the next. The emblem that follows in a clockwise direction (fig. 7) shows the interior view of a *camera obscura*, into which light enters through a hole, creating an upside-down and laterally inverted image on the opposite wall.

fig. 5: Heinrich Engelgrave, *LVCIS EVANGELICAE, SVB VELVM SACRORVM EMBLEMATVM RECONDITAE PARS TERTIA* […], Pars posterior, UB Rostock Fm-13 (Köln: J. Cnobbaert [widow], 1652), copper title.

fig. 6: Idem, detail.

The motto "Haec amat obscurum" ("it loves the dark") comes from Horace's *De arte poetica* v. 363 (65–68 BCE). The quotation is found in that passage (exceedingly frequently invoked in early modern poetics[50]) in which Horace compares poetry to painting ("ut pictura poesis" [v. 361]) and differentiates between darker, more difficult-to-access artefacts on the one hand and more lucid ones on the other. In the present emblematic-intermedial context, one is dealing with a (certainly intended) ambiguity of the accompanying motto. For the formulation can refer both to the light (*lux*), which loves the darkness in the camera because it is thus enabled to generate an image, and to the camera, which loves the darkness prevailing in it because it is the prerequisite for the production of an image – similar to the way *obscuritas* is the essential feature of the emblematic invention and production of an image.

The symbol at the bottom right (fig. 8) shows the sun, hidden by a cloud but nevertheless emitting rays of light, whereby the motto "Volet haec sub nube videri" ("it wants to be seen under a cloud") also taken (and slightly modified[51]) from Horace, *De arte poetica* v. 363 is to be interpreted in this specific emblematic context to the effect that the concealment of the sun by a cloud paradoxically creates the prerequisite for being able to look into the sun, which would not be possible without such concealment, but would entail the loss of sight. Here, the dialectic of the invisible God may come to mind, the sight of whom would be lethal (cf. Exod 33:20) and who, by means of concealment in the God-man Christ, becomes manifest and perceptible to the human sense of sight (cf. John 1:18). The last emblem (lower left) depicts a bird sitting on a branch with the sun shining

50 On this, cf., e.g., Seraina Plotke, *Gereimte Bilder. Visuelle Poesie im 17. Jahrhundert* (München: Fink, 2009), 111–125.

51 "luce" was replaced by "nube."

fig. 7: Idem, detail.

on it from behind (fig. 9). The motto ("Ceruice refulsit" ["it shone on her neck"]) comes from Vergil (70–19 BCE), *Aeneis* 1.402 – a passage without the knowledge of which interpreting the emblem can hardly succeed. It tells the story of Aeneas, who meets his mother, the goddess of love, Venus, for the first time – hidden in the form of a girl on the hunt. Aeneas recognizes Venus only at their parting, when her neck shines pink with unearthly light ("avertens rosea cervice refulsit"), whereupon he reproachfully asks her why she deceives him with false images ("quid natum totiens, crudelis tu quoque, falsis | ludis imaginibus?" [1.407–408]).

ENGELG
is IESV.
TERTIA
letior.
PARS

volet hæc sub naθe videri   Horat. de

fig. 8: Idem, detail.

Thus, to be decoded are (1) the four emblem medallions in the title copperplate engraving of Engelgrave's *Lux Evangelica*, also with regard to the question of how their motifs, all taken from the ancient pagan tradition (Horace, Virgil, Ovid), are to be interpreted as a self-reflection of emblematic art; (2) the symbols of the evangelists; (3) the light-giving Holy Scripture presented by them; (4) the Holy Spirit who floats down from heaven in the form of a dove, which itself is to be deciphered, and brings the divine life with him, i. e., provides enlightenment. The paragon precondition for the hermeneutical accomplishment of this complex decoding process is therefore the medium light (*lux*) provided by the third person of the Trinity as mediator. Behind this work of the Holy Spirit, who alone can claim to be able to provide true enlightenment, the intention of Engelgrave's work, noted on the *velum* and formulated in the title, clearly falls short. For the title announces that in this work the evan-

fig. 9: Idem, detail.

gelical light (*lux evangelica*) hidden under the curtain of sacred symbols is "varie" (varied) "adumbrata," i. e., not fully brought to light, but rather shaded or sketched. In this, an eschatological reflection comes to bear regarding the limits of performance and the provisionality with which biblical exegesis must come to terms until the Judgment Day.

Incidentally, it is by no means insignificant that the title copperplate's pictorial composition does not even hint at the Roman magisterium, which according to the Catholic – and especially Jesuit – opinion has the highest and thus ultimate authority in matters of biblical exegesis. At no point, moreover, is the Biblia Vulgata named as the canonical version of the Holy Scripture (according to Catholic conviction), which is why the engraving can be classified as non-denominational.

ESCHATOLOGICAL PERMANENCE OF INTERMEDIALITY AND ITS PRE-EXISTENT FOUNDATION IN THE INNER-TRINITARIAN INTER-MEDIALITY

It would be a misunderstanding to think that, according to the early modern view of things, with the future realization of the *visio beatifica* a situation of total immediacy, i. e., amediality or immediality, will arise between God and man. However, this is not the case since the media of music and spiritual song, as well as spiritual poetry connected with them, and of course Hebrew as the divine original language have a perpetual-eternal relevance. Furthermore, however, there is an aspect of fundamental importance with regard to the specifically eschatological-spiritual intermediality of the *visio beatifica* which is reflected in particular in spiritual emblematics:[52] According to early modern conviction, in the reciprocal vision of God and human beings, notwithstanding the *unio mystica* connecting them, which is conceived as a relational (i. e., medially determined) *unio spiritualis*, there remains an "in-between" (τὸ μεταξύ). This "in-between" is not only bridged by the Holy Spirit as *nexus*, consequently mediatorial, but decisively also by the media of mutual gazes that are made possible by the medium of divine light in the first place. Here, according to the early modern

view, the creative gaze of God has the task of permanently seeing the *imago Dei* in man and thus granting him eternal life and maintaining him therein. This means, however, that both the mediality of the gaze and that of the image have an ongoing and fundamental relevance in eternity as "time without time."

Undoubtedly, the multifaceted operationalization, theologization, and eschatologization of the understanding of media, which ultimately goes back to Aristotle, are reflected here. According to this, all entities are considered media, which in the Aristotelian sense function as "in-between" (τὸ μεταξύ[53]) and in this respect are to be regarded as the absolute constituents of mediation, communication, and perception.[54] This results in a broad understanding of media that is characterized by the conviction that entirely immaterial media do not exist.[55] Rather, a scaling of medial materiality should be expected. This is concretized in the fact that according to the Aristotelian view and according to the common view held in early modern times, light and air (as *conditiones sine quibus non* of visual, auditory, and olfactory perception) and consequently phenomena such as sound, the visible, the smellable, and the touchable also are to be understood as media.[56] According to this conception, the mediality of the (human) body is also not in question, which Aristotle defines as τὸ μεταξύ between tactility and affection (πάθος).[57] This

---

52 Cf. Steiger (note 1), 2:20.

53 Aristotle, *De an.* 423a.

54 Cf. Fritz Heider, *Ding und Medium* (Berlin: Kadmos, 2005; 1st ed. 1926), 32–33 *passim*.

55 Cf. Emmanuel Alloa, "Metaxy oder: Warum es keine immateriellen Medien gibt," in *Imaginäre Medialität / immaterielle Medien*, ed. Gertrud Koch, Kirsten Maar, Fiona McGovern (München: Fink, 2012),

13–34, here 20. Cf. further Georg Christoph Tholen, "Dazwischen – Die Medialität der Medien. Eine Skizze in vier Abschnitten," in *Medienbewegungen. Praktiken der Bezugnahme*, ed. Ludwig Jäger, Gisela Fehrmann, Meike Adam, Mediologie 18 (Paderborn: Fink, 2012), 43–62.

56 Cf. Aristotle, *De an.* 423b.

57 Cf. Aristotle, *De an.* 423b.

conception was received strongly in late scholasticism as well as in the early modern period and was especially formulated in the context of a theologically highly virulent discourse on the body-soul unity of the human being (including the one resurrected to eternal life). According to this understanding of media, it must be made clear that there can be no immediateness of God (by the way, not even in the inner-Trinitarian process),[58] if even with regard to the definition of the heavenly mystical union and the *beata visio*, it is necessary to speak of medial realities such as divine light, Holy Spirit, image of God, music, singing, and gazing. In this context, it is also import that, as Johann Conrad Dannhauer (1603–1666)[59] points out, those who are resurrected to eternal life will be like the angels. But just as the cherubim in God's throne room must cover their eyes with two of their six wings to be able to bear the radiance of God's light and perceive it through the "covering" (Isa 6:2), as Dannhauer says, so too the resurrected will have to guard their eyes from the *gloria* (δόξα) of God, which can never be fully perceived.[60] From this it becomes clear that the *beata visio* not only pre-supposes the mediality of the reciprocal gaze, but is moreover co-determined by medial interruption, within which the mediality of the human body is also of central concern.

If, therefore, the endeavor to tentatively and proleptically come as close as possible to the eschatological unraveling that will occur in the vision of God determines the cultivation of spiritual intermediality, including specifically emblematic intermediality that was particularly striking and intensified in the early modern period, then it is already recognizable in this foresight that the communicative sociality of those resurrected to eternal life will also be characterized by spiritual intermediality. However, as already mentioned, this will come to pass with the distinctions that the difference between horizontal and vertical intermediality will be abolished and the ability of people to recognize will be an undreamt-of higher and no longer fragmentary one, since they (according to 1 Cor 13:12) will recognize in being recognized by God, i.e., in the God-man interpersonality.

At this point, within the framework of eschatology, a protological factuality proves itself,

---

58 On this, cf. Philipp Stoellger, "Gott als Medium und der Traum der Gottunmittelbarkeit," in *Das Letzte – der Erste. Gott denken. Festschrift für Ingolf U. Dalferth zum 70. Geburtstag*, ed. Hans-Peter Großhans, Michael Moxter, Philipp Stoellger (Tübingen: Mohr Siebeck, 2018), 351–393, esp. 392–393 as well as Philipp Stoellger, "Reformation als Reformatierung der Medialität im Namen der Gottunmittelbarkeit," in *Reformation und Medien. Zu den intermedialen Wirkungen der Reformation*, ed. Johann Anselm Steiger, Reformation heute 4 (Leipzig: Evangelische Verlagsanstalt, 2018), 35–62, esp. 52–59.

59 Cf. Armin Wenz, "Dannhauer, Johann Conrad," in *Frühe Neuzeit in Deutschland 1620–1720. Literaturwissenschaftliches Verfasserlexikon*, ed. Stefanie Arend, Bernhard Jahn, Jörg Robert, Robert Seidel, Johann Anselm Steiger, Stefan Tilg, Friedrich Vollhardt (Berlin and Boston: de Gruyter, 2020), 2:460–476. Cf. further Daniel Bolliger, *Methodus als Lebensweg bei Johann Conrad Dannhauer. Existentialisierung der Dialektik in der lutherischen Orthodoxie*, Historia Hermeneutica, Series Studia 15 (Berlin and Boston: de Gruyter, 2020).

60 Johann Conrad Dannhauer, *CATECHJSMVS MJLCH Oder Der Erklärung deß Christlichen Catechismi/ Erster Theil/ Begreiffend die Lehr deß Catechismi ins gemein/ vnd die Erste Taffel deß Gesetzes der Heiligen zehen Gebott Gottes/ Zu Straßburg im Münster der Gemeine Gottes vorgetragen/ auffs new vbersehen/ gebessert/ vnd auff begehren in Truck gegeben [...]*, BSB München 2065 e-1/3 (Straßburg: F. Sporr, 1642), 282.

namely the fact that all spiritual intermediality has its origin in the pre-existent inner-divine, i.e., inner-Trinitarian intermediality. For the protomedium, Christ, is already to be regarded as a medial entity within the divine Trinity in which (*ad intra*) the three persons (God the Father, the Son, and the Holy Spirit) stand in mutual relations to each other. The same applies to the Holy Spirit, only with the difference that the second person of the Trinity is generated (note created) from eternity by the first, whereas the Holy Spirit proceeds from the first and the second persons. This intra-Trinitarian intermediality is accounted for when Christ is referred to, with François Turrettini (1623–1687), as "medius"[61] between the Father and the Spirit. According to the approach of Aurelius Augustine (354–430), which was recognized across denominational boundaries in the early modern period, the Holy Spirit has a comparable intermedial role within the Trinity, insofar as he functions as a *nexus* or *vinculum* between Father and Son. That with regard to the immanent Trinity the intermedial logic may be considered as a matrix thought becomes clear in the theologumenon of the procession (*processio*) of the Spirit from the Father and the Son (*filioque*). This intermedial logic also relates to the so-called economic doctrine of the Trinity – not only when it is emphasized that the three persons of the Trinity always work together externally (*ad extra*), but also when, for example, Zacharias Ursinus (1534–1583) calls the Holy Spirit a "vinculum […] intermedium"[62] between Christ who is seated at the right hand of God and the believers.

All photographs © Johann Anselm Steiger.

61 François Turrettini, *INSTITUTIO THEOLOGIAE ELENCTICAE, IN QUA STATUS CONTROVERSIAE PERSPICUE exponitur, Praecipua ORTHODOXORUM ARGUMENTA proponuntur, & vindicantur, & FONTES SOLUTIONUM aperiuntur*. […] *PARS SECUNDA*, SUB Göttingen 8 TH TH I, 568/47:2 (Leiden, Utrecht: F. Haring and E. Voskuyl, 1696), 407.

62 Zacharias Ursinus, *Volumen Tractationum Theologicarum: In quibus pleraque Christianae Religionis capita* […] *ex Dei verbo explicantur* […]. *Omnia nunc primùm, ex ipso autographo autoris, fideliter in lucem edita.* […], BSB München 2 Polem. 212 (Neustadt: Harnisch, 1584), 648.